THE LITTLE
HERB
COOKBOOK

THE LITTLE
HERB
COOKBOOK

SMITHMARK

This edition first published in 1996 by
SMITHMARK Publishers
a division of US Media Holdings Inc.
16 East 32nd Street
New York, NY 10016

Produced by
Anness Publishing Limited
1 Boundary Row
London SE1 8HP

SMITHMARK books are available for bulk purchase for
sales promotion and for premium use. For details write or
call the manager of special sales, SMITHMARK
Publishers, 16 East 32nd Street,
New York, NY 10016; (212 532 6600)

ISBN 0-8317-7429-0

Publisher Joanna Lorenz
Senior Cookery Editor Linda Fraser
Assistant Editor Emma Brown
Designers Patrick McLeavey & Jo Brewer
Illustrator Anna Koska
Photographer Michelle Garrett
Recipes Katherine Richmond
Food for photography Liz Trigg

10 9 8 7 6 5 4 3 2 1

Printed in Singapore by
Star Standard Industries Pte Ltd

Contents

Introduction

One of the most rewarding ways of flavoring food — and making a familiar dish quite unique — is by the careful use of herbs. There's something very satisfying about stepping outside on a warm, summer evening and cutting fresh chives, chervil and young sorrel leaves to add to a green salad, or big bunches of parsley for an authentic tabbouleh. Reach for a couple of bay leaves to garnish a terrine or flavor a winter stew, and you are instantly transported back to the sunny morning when you picked them, and hung them to dry in your kitchen.

Most herbs are easy to grow, demanding little more than a sunny position and light, well-drained soil. Whether you have a garden plot or just a few herbs on the window sill, being able to pick your own herbs and use them instantly, when the essential oils are at their most flavorsome, is richly rewarding. This has been recognized by most supermarkets, which now sell several varieties of growing herbs.

Dried herbs are more pungent than their fresh counterparts. You only need one-third to half the quantity. This can be a drawback; dried herbs you rarely use may have lost much of their flavor by the time the jar is empty, so store them carefully, away from direct sunlight, and check the jars regularly. Throw away any herbs that have become tasteless or musty.

Our ancestors valued herbs highly for medicinal purposes, as a means of flavoring and preserving food, and for their natural beauty and scent. They created beautiful herb gardens, often laid out as wheels or ladders, and hedged with lavender or box. In addition to culinary herbs, they cultivated varieties specifically for their healing properties, to be made into potions, salves or soothing foot baths. Some herbs, such as anise and dill seed, were regarded as being good for the digestion. Dill seed was traditionally cooked with cabbage for that reason.

In recent years, there has been a resurgence of interest in herbs, both as natural remedies and in cooking. As cooks become more cosmopolitan, herbs like cilantro and lemon grass are becoming increasingly popular, and while parsley and mint still hold the high ground, we now expect to be able to buy several varieties of these

familiar herbs, as well as sage, thyme, marjoram, rosemary, oregano, chives and all the other aromatics.

The best way to familiarize yourself with culinary herbs is to be adventurous and to experiment. Although some of the herbs have a natural affinity for certain foods (rosemary with lamb; sage with pork; dill with fish; basil with tomatoes), it is often the unexpected combination that produces the most exciting results. Duck with Red Plums & Cilantro, for instance, or Chicken with Blackberries & Lemon Balm. These are just two of the many delicious recipes that feature in *The Little Herb Cookbook*, from soups, savories and salads to sweet surprises and refreshing drinks, issuing an open invitation to explore the wonderful world of culinary herbs.

7

Kitchen Herbs

BASIL
Known for its affinity with tomatoes, basil is also excellent with fish, pasta and egg dishes.

DILL
The leaves are used with fish and the seeds for cabbage dishes, marinades and pickles.

BAY
The dried leaves are used in stews, soups, casseroles and milk desserts.

8

CHIVES
Use plain or garlic chives as a garnish for soups and salads, with cream cheese or omelets.

CILANTRO
The leaves add a hint of spice to salads, vegetables, and some desserts. Try coriander seeds in curries, with roast pork and casseroles.

MARJORAM
A cultivated variety of oregano, with a milder flavor. Use with lamb, poultry, in stuffings and egg and cheese dishes.

MINT
Don't just use this refreshing herb in mint sauce. Try it sprinkled over salads, tomato soup or grapefruit.

OREGANO

Although known as the "pizza herb," oregano is not just used for this purpose. It is widely used in Italian cooking, and goes well with meats, tomatoes, zucchini, eggs and cheese.

PARSLEY

Curly or Italian, parsley has a wonderful, clean taste. Try it in salads, soups, stuffings and deep-fried as a special garnish.

ROSEMARY

The leaves of this pungent herb look like tiny pine needles. Use sparingly in soups, stews or vegetable dishes, or insert, with slivers of garlic, in lamb before roasting.

SAGE

These soft, silky gray-green leaves are especially good with pork, in stuffings (most commonly in combination with onion) and with pan-fried liver.

9

TARRAGON

Used to flavor vinegar and for fish dishes, sauces (such as Béarnaise) and salad dressings.

THYME

The tiny leaves are widely used in stuffings, meat loaves, tomato dishes and with eggs and cheese.

Techniques

PICKING

Pick herbs often. Early in the morning is best. Remove the outer leaves of parsley and chervil first, and pick out the tops of basil frequently to stop the plant flowering too early.

DRYING

Herbs are best dried naturally, hung in an airy passageway or kitchen, or laid on a wire rack. They can also be dried overnight in an oven heated to the lowest temperature, then turned off. Strip off the dried leaves from the stems, and store whole or crumbled in airtight jars.

FREEZING

Chopped or finely cut tarragon, mint, chives and basil all freeze well. Pack them in ice cube trays, fill with water, and freeze until solid. Then put in plastic wrap, and label. Return to the freezer for up to 6 months.

CHOPPING

Use either a sharp, broad-bladed knife or a mezzaluna (a curved blade with a handle at each end) when chopping up herbs. The easiest way to chop small amounts of parsley and similar herbs is to put them in a cup, and cut them using a pair of sharp scissors.

Using Herbs

HERB VINEGAR
See the recipe for Rosemary Vinegar (page 48) for inspiration. Use tarragon, basil or lemon thyme instead of the rosemary, if you prefer.

HERB BUTTER
Top broiled fish or steaks with herb butter: mix 4 tbsp finely chopped parsley, dill and chervil with ½ cup softened butter. Shape into a roll, wrap and chill. Cut the butter into slices for serving.

HERB BAKES
Add chopped herbs to biscuit mixes (see Cheese & Marjoram Biscuits, page 56), breads or savory crackers.

BOUQUET GARNI
Make your own bouquet garni by tying a bay leaf and a sprig each of thyme, marjoram and parsley together.

11

TIME-SAVING TIP
To dry fresh herbs in the microwave, spread the clean sprigs in an even layer between several paper towels, and microwave on High (100% power) for 2 minutes. Rearrange the herbs, cover with fresh paper towels, and cook for about 2 minutes more, checking the herbs every 30 seconds and removing them from the microwave as soon as they appear dry. Let cool, and dry completely. Never leave the microwave unattended when drying herbs.

Appetizers &
Light Lunches

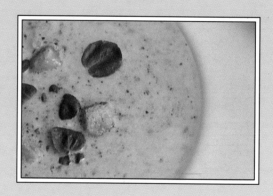

Herb & Chili Gazpacho

INGREDIENTS

2½ pounds ripe tomatoes
2 onions
2 green bell peppers
1 large cucumber
1 green chili, seeded
2 tablespoons red wine vinegar
1 tablespoon balsamic vinegar
2 tablespoons olive oil
1 garlic clove, crushed
1¼ cups tomato juice
2 tablespoons tomato paste
2 tablespoons chopped mixed fresh herbs, plus
extra to garnish
salt and ground black pepper

SERVES 6

13

1 Set aside about a quarter of the tomatoes, onions, green bell peppers and the cucumber. Coarsely chop the remaining vegetables, including the chili, and place in a food processor or blender. Add the remaining ingredients, with salt and pepper to taste. Process finely, and pour into a bowl. Cover and chill.

2 Carefully chop all the reserved vegetables into fine dice, and place in a separate bowl for serving with the soup. Alternatively, place the diced vegetables in individual bowls. Serve the soup in chilled bowls, adding one or two crushed ice cubes to each portion. Garnish with herbs.

Pear & Watercress Soup with Blue Cheese Croûtons

INGREDIENTS

1 bunch watercress
4 pears, sliced
3¾ cups chicken broth, preferably homemade
½ cup heavy cream
juice of 1 lime
salt and ground black pepper
CROUTONS
2 tablespoons butter
1 tablespoon olive oil
3 cups cubed stale bread
1 cup crumbled blue cheese

SERVES 6

I Set aside about a third of the watercress leaves. Place the rest of the watercress leaves and the stalks in a saucepan with the pears, broth and a little salt and pepper. Simmer for 15–20 minutes, until the pears are tender. Transfer the mixture to a food processor or blender. Keeping back some of the reserved watercress leaves for garnishing, add the rest to the pear mixture, and immediately process until smooth.

2 Scrape the mixture into a clean saucepan. Stir in the cream and lime juice, mixing thoroughly. Season again to taste. Set the pan aside.

3 To make the croûtons, melt the butter with the oil in a frying pan, and fry the bread cubes until golden brown. Drain well on paper towels. Preheat the broiler. Spread the croûtons out on a broiler pan, sprinkle the crumbled cheese over the top, and heat under a hot broiler until bubbling.

4 Reheat the soup over a low heat, stirring occasionally until warmed through. Do not allow the soup to approach boiling point, or it will curdle. Serve in heated bowls, topped with the croûtons and reserved watercress leaves.

COOK'S TIP
The basis of all soups is a good fresh broth, which should be homemade if possible. Broths can be frozen for up to two months — boil the broth over a high heat to reduce it by half, then cool. Freeze in ice cube trays.

Smoked Trout with Minted Grapefruit

1 Toss the lettuce leaves with the lemon juice and half the chopped mint in a bowl. Tuck the smoked trout slices among the leaves, then carefully arrange  on a serving plate. Add the segments of grapefruit, and garnish the salad with mint leaves.

2 Mix the remaining chopped mint with the mayonnaise in a small bowl. Garnish the mayonnaise with two or three mint leaves, and serve it with the salad.

INGREDIENTS

1 lollo rosso lettuce, separated into leaves
1 tablespoon lemon juice
2 tablespoons chopped fresh mint
1 pound smoked trout, skinned, boned and sliced
2 grapefruit, peeled and segmented
½ cup good bottled mayonnaise
mint leaves, to garnish

SERVES 4

VARIATION
Try this alternative for a delicious change. Use smoked mackerel instead of trout, and add 1 tablespoon horseradish sauce to the mayonnaise. Serve with the salad.

Warm Chicken Salad with Cilantro Dressing

INGREDIENTS

4 chicken breasts, boned and skinned
1 1/2 cups snow peas
2 heads lollo rosso or feuille de chêne,
separated into leaves
3 carrots, cut into small matchsticks
1 1/2 cups sliced button mushrooms
6 bacon rashers, broiled and crumbled
fresh cilantro leaves, to garnish
DRESSING
1/2 cup lemon juice
2 tablespoons whole-grain mustard
1 cup olive oil
5 tablespoons sesame oil
1 teaspoon coriander seeds, crushed

SERVES 6

2 Cook the snow peas for 2 minutes in boiling water, then drain, cool under cold running water, and pat dry. Arrange the lettuce leaves with the other salad ingredients on serving dishes. Sprinkle with the bacon.

3 Drain the chicken breasts, discarding the dressing used as a marinade. Broil them until cooked through, then slice on the diagonal into quite thin pieces. Divide among the portions of salad. Drizzle a little of the reserved dressing over each serving, and sprinkle over some cilantro leaves. Serve any remaining dressing separately.

17

1 Mix together the dressing ingredients. Place the chicken breasts in a shallow dish, and pour on half the dressing. Cover the dish. Let marinate in a cool place for several hours, or chill overnight. Reserve the remaining dressing until required.

Potted Salmon with Lemon & Dill

INGREDIENTS

12 ounces cooked salmon, skinned
⅔ cup butter, softened
grated rind and juice of 1 large lemon
2 teaspoons chopped fresh dill
¾ cup sliced almonds, coarsely chopped
salt and ground black pepper
dill sprigs, to garnish
crudités, such as baby corn, fennel wedges,
celery and carrot sticks, to serve

SERVES 6

18

1 Flake the salmon into a bowl, taking care to remove any bones. Place in a food processor or blender with two-thirds of the butter. Add the lemon rind and juice, half

the chopped fresh dill, and salt and pepper to taste. Process the mixture until quite smooth in texture.

2 Mix in all the sliced almonds. Check for seasoning, and adjust if necessary. Scrape the mixture from the food processor or blender into ramekins, leveling

the surface of each with the back of a spoon if you intend to seal the salmon with butter.

3 Seal the potted salmon with butter, if you like: sprinkle the remaining dill over the top of each ramekin, then melt the remaining butter. Set aside until the solids separate. Carefully spoon a little of the clarified butter over each ramekin to seal the potted salmon. Chill until set. Garnish with dill sprigs, and serve with the crudités.

Normandy Fish with Parsley & Dill

INGREDIENTS

2¼ pounds white fish fillets
1 tablespoon chopped parsley
3 cups button mushrooms
8-ounce can tomatoes
2 cups cider
2 teaspoons flour
1 tablespoon butter
1 large bunch dill
3 tablespoons Calvados
salt and ground black pepper
parsley leaves, to garnish

SERVES 4

2 Heat the cider in a saucepan to simmering point. Work the flour into the butter to make a paste, then stir it into the cider, a little at a time, making sure that each piece is absorbed before adding the next. Cook, stirring, until the cider has thickened slightly.

1 Preheat the oven to 350°F. Skin the fish carefully with a sharp knife, then chop it coarsely, and place it in a casserole. Add the chopped parsley, button mushrooms and tomatoes, with the can juices. Season with salt and pepper to taste.

3 Set aside a few dill sprigs for the garnish. Chop the remaining dill, and stir it into the cider mixture with the Calvados. Pour over the fish mixture, cover, and bake for about 30 minutes. Serve garnished with the dill sprigs and a few parsley leaves.

Meat & Poultry Dishes

Beef with Herby Orange Mustard

INGREDIENTS

3 oranges
3 tablespoons oil
1 1/2 pounds braising steak, cubed
2 onions, chopped
1 garlic clove, crushed
2 tablespoons flour
1 1/4 cups beef broth
1 tablespoon tomato paste
3 tablespoons Grand Marnier
1 tablespoon maple syrup
1 cup sliced mushrooms
2 tablespoons finely chopped mixed fresh herbs,
such as thyme and chives
3 tablespoons Dijon mustard
salt and ground black pepper

SERVES 4

1 Cut one orange in half. Slice one half thinly, and set the slices aside. Pare the other two oranges very thinly, and cut the pared rind into thin strips. Squeeze the pared oranges, and reserve the juice.

2 Preheat the oven to 350°F. Heat the oil in a flameproof casserole, and fry the beef cubes until sealed on all sides. Transfer to a bowl, and set aside. Add the onions and garlic to the casserole, and fry until softened. Stir in the flour. Cook for 1 minute, then gradually stir in the broth.

3 Stir the mixture until it boils and thickens, then return the beef to the casserole, and stir in the orange rind strips and orange juice, tomato paste, Grand Marnier and maple syrup. Add salt and pepper to taste. Cover, and cook in the oven for about 1 1/2 hours, until the beef is just tender. Add the sliced mushrooms, and return the casserole to the oven for 30 minutes more.

4 Meanwhile, grate all the rind from the remaining 1/2 orange into a bowl. Squeeze in the orange juice. Add the herbs and mustard, and mix well. Serve the beef garnished with the reserved orange slices. Offer the herby orange mustard separately. Creamy mashed potato makes an excellent accompaniment.

21

Roast Pork with Sage & Marjoram

INGREDIENTS

6-pound leg of pork
3 tablespoons sage leaves
1 tablespoon marjoram leaves
3 tablespoons chopped celery leaves
4 tablespoons cider
salt and ground black pepper
APPLE PUREE
1 tablespoon butter
2 eating apples
2 bananas
1 tablespoon Calvados

SERVES 8

I Preheat the oven to 350°F. Strip off the rind from the pork, leaving an even layer of fat. Cut a piece of foil large enough to enclose the pork, and place the pork in the center. In a bowl, mix the sage, marjoram and celery leaves together. Cover the pork fat with the herb mixture, season to taste, and wrap tightly. Support the foil package in a roasting pan (this can be done by placing a wire rack over the pan.) Roast for 2 hours.

2 Fold back the foil, and drizzle the cider over the pork, taking care not to disturb the herb coating. Continue cooking for 1–1½ hours, until a small, sharp knife pressed into the thickest part of the joint produces clear juices.

3 Make the apple purée. Melt the butter in a small saucepan. Peel, quarter and core the apples, and slice them into the pan. Turn to coat the slices in butter, then slice the bananas into the pan. Sauté the fruit for 2 minutes. Add the Calvados, and set it alight. When the flames die down, remove the mixture from the heat, and purée it in a food processor or blender. Spoon the purée into a small pitcher or bowl, and serve with the roast pork.

COOK'S TIP
Herbs are widely used in cooking to add extra flavor to a dish. Although sage and marjoram are classic accompaniments to pork, thyme or rosemary would be equally good.

Lamb Pie with Pear, Ginger & Mint Sauce

INGREDIENTS

1 boned mid-loin of lamb, about 2¼ pounds
after boning
1 tablespoon oil
2 tablespoons butter, plus extra for greasing
8 large sheets filo pastry
salt and ground black pepper
Italian parsley, to garnish
STUFFING & SAUCE
1 small onion, chopped
1 tablespoon butter
1 cup whole wheat bread crumbs
grated rind of 1 lemon
¼ teaspoon ground ginger
14-ounce can pears
1 egg, beaten
2 teaspoons finely chopped fresh mint, plus
a small sprig, to garnish

SERVES 6

1 Make the stuffing. Fry the onion in the butter until soft. Pour into a bowl, and add the bread crumbs, lemon rind and ginger. Drain the pears, reserving the juice and half the fruit. Chop the remaining pears, and add them to the mixture. Season, and bind with the egg. Spread the loin out flat, fat-side down, and season. Place the stuffing along the middle of the loin, and roll up carefully.

2 Holding the meat firmly, close the opening with a trussing needle threaded with string. Heat the oil in a heavy-based frying pan, and brown the roll slowly on all sides, until well colored. Let cool, and store in the fridge until needed.

3 Preheat the oven to 400°F. Melt the butter. Keeping the remainder of the filo covered, brush two sheets with a little butter. Overlap by about 5 inches to make a square. Place the next two sheets on top, and brush with butter. Continue until all the filo has been used.

4 Remove the string from the lamb, and place the roll diagonally across one corner of the pastry, so that it sits within the pastry square, without over-hanging the edges. Fold the corner of the pastry over the lamb, fold in the sides, and brush with melted butter. Roll up neatly. Place the roll join-side down on a greased baking sheet, and bake for 40 minutes, covering it with foil if it browns too rapidly and looks as if it might burn.

5 Meanwhile, make the sauce. Purée the reserved pears, juice and mint. Pour into a sauce-boat, and garnish with a mint sprig. Place the lamb on a platter, garnish with Italian parsley, and serve with the pear, ginger and mint sauce.

Chicken with Blackberries & Lemon Balm

INGREDIENTS

4 chicken breasts, partly boned
2 tablespoons butter
1 tablespoon sunflower oil
4 tablespoons flour
⅔ cup red wine
⅔ cup chicken broth
grated rind and juice of ½ orange
3 lemon balm sprigs, finely chopped
⅔ cup heavy cream
1 egg yolk
⅔ cup fresh blackberries
salt and ground black pepper
GARNISH
lemon balm sprigs
⅓ cup fresh blackberries

SERVES 4

1 Preheat the oven to 350°F. Trim the chicken breasts, removing any skin. Heat the butter and oil in a large frying pan. Fry the chicken until sealed on all sides, then transfer to a casserole.

2 Stir the flour into the fat remaining in the frying pan. Cook for 1 minute, then gradually stir in the wine and broth. Heat, stirring until the sauce thickens. Add the orange rind and juice, and also the chopped lemon balm. Pour over the chicken. Cover the casserole, and cook in the oven for 40 minutes.

3 Lightly whisk the cream with the egg yolk in a bowl. Whisk in some of the liquid from the casserole, then stir the contents of the bowl into the casserole. Add

the blackberries. Cover, and cook for 10–15 minutes more. Serve the chicken garnished with the lemon balm and fresh blackberries.

Chicken with Sloe Gin & Juniper

INGREDIENTS

2 tablespoons butter
2 tablespoons sunflower oil
8 chicken breasts, boned and skinned
4 carrots, sliced
1 garlic clove, crushed
1 tablespoon finely chopped parsley
4 tablespoons chicken broth
4 tablespoons red wine
4 tablespoons sloe gin
1 teaspoon crushed juniper berries
salt and ground black pepper
shredded fresh basil, to garnish

SERVES 8

27

1 Melt the butter with the oil in a large frying pan. Fry the chicken breasts until they are brown on all sides. Then transfer to a shallow pan or casserole.

2 Cook the carrots in a saucepan of boiling, lightly salted water until tender. Drain and place in a food processor or blender. Add the garlic, parsley, broth, wine, gin and juniper berries.

3 Process the carrot mixture to a smooth purée. If the mixture seems too thick, thin it with a little more red wine or water. Pour the sauce over the top of the chicken, then cover, and simmer over a low heat for about 15 minutes, or until the chicken is cooked through. Season to taste. Transfer to a serving bowl, and serve immediately, garnished with the shredded fresh basil.

Turkey with Fig & Mint Sauce

1 Place the figs in a saucepan with the wine. Bring to a boil, lower the heat, and simmer very gently for about 1 hour. Then let cool, and chill overnight.

2 Melt the butter in a frying pan. Fry the turkey fillets until they are cooked right through. Remove them from the pan, cover, and keep hot. Drain any fat from the pan, and pour in the juice from the figs. Bring to a boil, and reduce rapidly until about ⅔ cup of the juice remains.

3 Add the marmalade to the pan, together with the chopped mint and the lemon juice. Simmer for a few minutes, then add salt and pepper to taste.

4 When the sauce is thick and shiny, add the figs, and allow to heat through for a couple of minutes. Then pour the sauce over the turkey fillets, and serve garnished with the mint sprigs.

28

INGREDIENTS

1 pound dried figs
½ bottle sweet, fruity white wine
1 tablespoon butter
4 turkey fillets, 6-8 ounces each
2 tablespoons dark orange marmalade
10 mint leaves, chopped
juice of ½ lemon
salt and ground black pepper
mint sprigs, to garnish

SERVES 4

Duck with Red Plums & Cilantro

INGREDIENTS

4 duck breasts, about 6 ounces each, skinned
2 teaspoons crushed stick cinnamon
¼ cup butter
1 tablespoon plum brandy or Cognac
1 cup chicken broth
1 cup heavy cream
6 red plums, pitted and sliced
6 cilantro sprigs, plus extra to garnish
salt and ground black pepper

SERVES 4

2 Add the broth and cream to the pan, and simmer gently until reduced and thickened. Taste the sauce, and add more salt and pepper if required.

3 Reserve a few plum slices for the garnish. Melt the remaining butter, and fry the plums with the cilantro sprigs for just long enough to cook the fruit through.

4 Place the duck breasts on individual plates. Pour a little of the sauce around each portion, and divide the plum slices among the plates. Garnish with the cilantro, and serve at once.

29

1 Preheat the oven to 375°F. Score the duck breasts, and sprinkle lightly with salt. Press the crushed cinnamon on both sides of the duck breasts. Melt half the butter in a large frying pan. Fry the duck breasts on both sides to seal, then place them in an ovenproof dish. Pour over the pan juices. Bake for 6–7 minutes. Remove the dish from the oven, and return the contents to the cleaned frying pan. Add the brandy, and ignite. When the flames die down, remove the duck breasts. Keep them hot.

Vegetable Dishes
& Salads

Vegetable & Herb Kebabs with Green Peppercorn Sauce

INGREDIENTS

16 short or 8 long bamboo skewers, soaked in
water for about 30 minutes
8 flat mushrooms, halved
16 large basil leaves
16 cherry tomatoes
16 large mint leaves
16 chunks of zucchini
16 pieces of red bell pepper
green and purple basil sprigs, to garnish
BASTE
½ cup melted butter
1 clove garlic, peeled and crushed
1 tablespoon crushed green peppercorns
salt
GREEN PEPPERCORN SAUCE
¼ cup butter
3 tablespoons brandy
1 cup heavy cream
1 teaspoon green peppercorns

SERVES 4

1 Thread the vegetables on to the bamboo skewers, placing the basil leaves immediately next to the tomatoes, and wrapping the mint leaves around the zucchini pieces. Thread on one piece of each type of vegetable per skewer if using short skewers, or two pieces of each per skewer if using long skewers.

2 Preheat the broiler. Mix the baste ingredients together in a small bowl and brush over the kebabs so that they are thoroughly basted. Put the kebabs on a rack and place under the broiler. Cook for about 7–8 minutes, turning and basting regularly, until the vegetables are just tender.

3 Meanwhile, make the green peppercorn sauce. Heat the butter in a frying pan, then add the brandy and carefully light it. When the flames die down, stir in the cream and the peppercorns. Cook for approximately 2 minutes, stirring all the time.

4 When cooked, transfer the kebabs to serving plates and garnish with basil. Serve with the green peppercorn sauce.

Spinach, Walnut & Swiss Cheese Lasagne with Basil

INGREDIENTS

12 ounces no-need-to-precook spinach lasagne
2 tablespoons torn basil leaves
1 tablespoon chopped walnuts
WALNUT AND TOMATO SAUCE
3 tablespoons walnut oil
1 large onion, chopped
8 ounces celery root, finely chopped
14-ounce can chopped tomatoes
1 large garlic clove, finely chopped
1/2 teaspoon sugar
1 cup chopped walnuts
2/3 cup Dubonnet
salt and ground black pepper
SPINACH AND SWISS CHEESE SAUCE
1 pound frozen spinach, thawed
1/3 cup butter
2 tablespoons walnut oil
1 onion, chopped
3/4 cup flour
1 teaspoon mustard powder
5 cups milk
2 cups grated Swiss cheese
grated nutmeg

SERVES 8

1 First, make the walnut and tomato sauce. Heat the walnut oil in a saucepan, and sauté the onion and celery root for 8–10 minutes until softened. Meanwhile, purée the tomatoes with their juice in a food processor or blender. Add the garlic to the saucepan, and cook for about 1 minute. Then add the sugar, chopped walnuts, tomatoes and Dubonnet together with salt and pepper to taste. Simmer, uncovered, for 25 minutes.

2 Preheat the oven to 350°F. Make the spinach and Swiss cheese sauce. Purée the spinach. Melt the butter with the walnut oil in a saucepan, add the onion, and fry for 5 minutes, then stir in the flour. Cook for 1 minute more, then add the mustard powder and milk, stirring vigorously until the sauce boils and thickens. Remove the pan from the heat, and add three-quarters of the grated cheese. Stir in the puréed spinach, and season to taste with salt, pepper and nutmeg.

3 Spread a layer of the spinach and cheese sauce in an ovenproof dish, then add a little walnut and tomato sauce. Top with an even layer of lasagne. Continue layering the sauces and pasta in this way until the dish is full, ending with a layer of sauce. Sprinkle the remaining cheese and the walnuts over the top, and strew with basil. Bake for 45 minutes.

32

Broccoli & Cauliflower with Apple Mint Sauce

INGREDIENTS

4 large apple mint sprigs
2 tablespoons olive oil
1 large onion, chopped
2 large carrots, chopped
1 large garlic clove, crushed
1 tablespoon dill seeds
2 tablespoons flour
1¼ cups hard cider
1 pound broccoli florets
1 pound cauliflower florets
2 tablespoons soy sauce
2 teaspoons mint jelly

SERVES 4

1 Strip the apple mint leaves from the main stems. Heat the olive oil in a frying pan, and sauté the onion, carrots, crushed garlic, dill seeds and mint until the vegetables are almost tender. Stir in the flour, and cook for 1 minute, then gradually stir in the cider. Simmer until the sauce looks glossy.

2 Cook the broccoli and cauliflower in separate pans of boiling, salted water until tender. Drain, mix together, and keep hot in a serving dish. Meanwhile, purée the sauce with the soy sauce and mint jelly in a food processor or blender. Pour the mixture over the broccoli and cauliflower, and serve at once.

Zucchini & Carrot Ribbons

INGREDIENTS

1 large green bell pepper, seeded and diced
1 tablespoon sunflower oil
8 ounces Brie cheese
2 tablespoons sour cream
1 teaspoon lemon juice
4 tablespoons milk
2 teaspoons freshly ground black pepper
2 tablespoons finely chopped parsley, plus extra
to garnish
6 large zucchini
6 large carrots, peeled
salt and ground black pepper

SERVES 4

1 In a saucepan, sauté the green pepper in the oil until just tender. Remove with a slotted spoon, and set aside. Process all of the remaining ingredients,  except the zucchini and carrots, in a food processor or blender. Scrape the mixture into the clean saucepan, and stir in the green pepper. Set aside.

2 Use a vegetable peeler to slice the zucchini and carrots into long, thin strips. Place the zucchini and carrot strips in two separate saucepans, then add water to  cover. Bring to a boil. Lower the heat, and simmer for 3 minutes until barely cooked. Drain.

3 Meanwhile, gently heat the green pepper sauce. When hot, pour it into a shallow vegetable dish. Add the zucchini and carrot strips to the dish, and toss lightly with the sauce until well mixed. Garnish with a little finely chopped parsley, and serve the dish at once.

35

Potato Salad with Rosemary Mayonnaise

INGREDIENTS

2¼ pounds new potatoes, in skins
pinch of salt
1¼ cups good bottled mayonnaise
6 rosemary leaves, finely chopped, plus extra
sprigs to garnish
pinch of black pepper
Italian parsley or mixed lettuce, to serve

SERVES 6

36

I Place the new potatoes in a large saucepan of salted water. Bring to a boil, and cook for 15 minutes or until tender. Do not overcook, or the potatoes will become mushy and collapse. Drain, and pour into a large bowl or colander to cool slightly.

2 Mix the mayonnaise with the chopped rosemary leaves and black pepper to taste. Spoon it over the potatoes while they are still warm, and mix together lightly to coat. Let cool, then serve on a bed of Italian parsley or mixed lettuce leaves, garnished with rosemary sprigs.

COOK'S TIP

For a special treat, use homemade mayonnaise. Place two egg yolks in a bowl with a pinch of mustard powder. Very gradually (a few drops at a time), beat in 1¼ cups vegetable or sunflower oil. If the mayonnaise becomes too thick, add a few drops of lemon juice. Season with salt and white pepper to taste. Mayonnaise can also be made in a food processor or blender — pulse in the oil.

Green Bean Salad with Savory

INGREDIENTS

1 pound green beans
2¼ pounds ripe tomatoes
3 scallions, coarsely sliced
1 tablespoon pine nuts
a few fresh savory sprigs
DRESSING
2 tablespoons extra virgin olive oil
juice of 1 lime
3 ounces dolcelatte cheese
1 garlic clove, crushed
salt and ground black pepper

SERVES 4

1 Prepare the dressing first, so that it can stand a while before use. Process the olive oil, lime juice, dolcelatte and crushed garlic in a food processor or blender until smooth. Pour into a pitcher or bowl, season to taste, and set aside.

2 Remove the ends from the beans. Cook in a saucepan of boiling, salted water until just tender. Drain the beans, and rinse under cold running water until cold. (This stops the cooking process and fixes the color.) Drain on paper towels. Slice the tomatoes, or, if they are fairly small, cut them into quarters.

3 Combine all the salad ingredients, except the pine nuts and savory, in a large bowl. Toss together with your hands. Pour the dressing over the top, and toss once again, or serve the dressing separately, if you prefer. Break the savory into tiny sprigs, and sprinkle over the salad, with the pine nuts, just before serving.

37

Desserts & Drinks

Chocolate Mint Truffle Filo Packages

INGREDIENTS

1 tablespoon very finely chopped mint
¾ cup ground almonds
2 ounces semisweet chocolate
2 eating apples
½ cup sour cream or ricotta cheese
9 large sheets filo pastry
6 tablespoons melted butter
1 tablespoon each confectioner's sugar and
cocoa powder, to dust

MAKES 18

1 Preheat the oven to 375°F. Grease two baking sheets. Mix the mint and almonds in a bowl. Grate in the chocolate. Peel and core the apples, and grate them into the bowl too. Stir in the sour cream or ricotta cheese. Cut the filo pastry into 18 3-inch squares, and cover with a clean cloth to prevent them from drying out.

2 Brush a square of filo with melted butter, top with a second square of filo, brush again with butter, then place a spoonful of the filling in the center. Bring up all  four corners, and twist to form a purse shape. Repeat to make about 18 filo packages.

3 Place the filo packages on the prepared baking sheets. Brush with the remaining melted butter, and bake for 10 minutes or until golden. Cool on wire racks, then dust with the confectioner's sugar, followed by the cocoa powder.

39

Summer Fruit Cake with Heartsease

INGREDIENTS

½ cup soft margarine, plus extra for greasing
½ cup sugar
2 teaspoons clear honey
1½ cups self-rising flour, plus extra
for dusting
½ teaspoon baking powder
2 eggs
2-4 tablespoons milk
1 tablespoon rose water
1 tablespoon Cointreau
confectioner's sugar, to dust
4 cups strawberries
whipped cream or custard sauce,
to serve (optional)
DECORATION
16 heartsease pansies
1 egg white
superfine sugar (see method)
strawberry leaves

SERVES 6–8

1 Crystallize the heartsease pansies by painting them with lightly beaten egg white, then sprinkling them with superfine sugar. Let dry on a wire rack. Preheat the oven to 375°F. Grease and lightly flour an ovenproof ring mold.

2 Place the soft margarine, sugar, honey, flour, baking powder and eggs in a large mixing bowl. Add 2 tablespoons of the milk, and beat well to combine. Add the rose water and the Cointreau, and mix well. Beat in the remaining milk, if necessary, to give a soft, dropping consistency.

3 Pour the mixture into the ring mold, and bake for 35–40 minutes, or until a cake tester inserted into the cake comes out clean — this indicates that it is cooked. Allow to stand for a few minutes, then turn out on to a serving plate. Let cool.

4 Sift confectioner's sugar over the cake. Fill the center with the strawberries, and place any extra around the edge. Decorate the serving plate with the crystallized heartsease flowers and some strawberry leaves. Serve the cake cut in thin slices, with whipped cream or custard sauce, if you like.

Iced Lemon Meringue Bombe with Mint Chocolate

INGREDIENTS

2 large lemons
⅔ cup sugar
⅔ cup whipping cream
2½ cups strained plain yogurt
2 large meringues, lightly crushed
3 mint sprigs
8 ounces good quality mint chocolate, grated

SERVES 6–8

42

I Pare the lemons thinly, taking care to remove none of the white pith. Chop the pared rind coarsely, and place it in a food processor or in a blender. Squeeze the lemons, and set the juice aside. Add the sugar to the lemon rind. Process finely, then add the cream, yogurt and lemon juice, and process thoroughly. Pour the mixture into a mixing bowl, and add the crushed meringues.

2 Reserve one of the mint sprigs for the decoration, and chop the rest finely. Add to the cream and lemon mixture. Pour into a 5 cup bombe mold. Freeze for 4 hours.

3 When the ice cream is solid, scoop out the middle and reserve. Set aside a little of the grated mint chocolate for decoration, then turn the rest into the hollow in the ice cream. Fill the hollow with the reserved ice cream and smooth flat. Return the bombe to the freezer for several hours.

4 To serve, dip the mold in very hot water for a few seconds to loosen the ice cream. Then hold a serving plate tightly over the top, and invert it. Gently remove the mold. Decorate with the reserved grated chocolate and mint sprig, and serve immediately.

COOK'S TIP

You can buy pre-made meringue or make your own. To make, whisk 2 egg whites until stiff, whisk in ¼ cup superfine sugar until stiff peaks form, then fold in another ¼ cup superfine sugar. Spread out on to a baking tray lined with parchment paper. Dry in an oven preheated to 300°F for about 45 minutes. Allow to cool before using.

Strawberry Punch with Herbs

INGREDIENTS

2 cups clear honey
4 quarts water
2 cups freshly squeezed lemon juice
3 tablespoons fresh rosemary leaves, plus
a few sprigs to decorate
8 cups sliced strawberries
2 cups freshly squeezed
lime juice
7½ cups sparkling mineral water
ice cubes
3-4 scented geranium leaves

SERVES ABOUT 30

44

I Combine the honey and 4 cups of the water with 4 tablespoons of the lemon juice in a large saucepan. Add the fresh rosemary leaves. Bring to a boil, stirring until all the honey is dissolved. Remove from the heat, and allow to stand until cool. Strain into a large punch bowl or pitcher.

2 Purée the strawberries by pressing them through a strainer into a bowl using a wooden spoon. Add the purée to the punch bowl with the rest of the water and the citrus juices. Stir gently. Just before serving, pour in the sparkling water, add the ice cubes, and float the geranium leaves and rosemary sprigs on the surface.

Citrus Mint Sparkler

INGREDIENTS

4 mint sprigs
½ teaspoon sugar
crushed ice
½ teaspoon lemon juice
2 tablespoons grapefruit juice
½ cup chilled tonic water
1-2 lemon slices, to decorate

SERVES I

1 Using a pestle and mortar, crush two of the mint sprigs with the sugar. Scrape the crushed mint into a glass. Fill the glass with crushed ice.

2 Add the lemon juice, grapefruit juice and tonic water. Stir gently, and decorate with the remaining mint sprigs and one or two lemon slices.

COOK'S TIP

If you prefer, make more than one glass at a time, and mix the ingredients in a large pitcher. For decoration, try freezing tiny sprigs of mint in ice cubes and adding to the drink.

Preserves & Dressings

Dill Pickles

INGREDIENTS

6 small cucumbers
2 cups water
4 cups white wine vinegar
½ cup salt
4-6 bay leaves
3 tablespoons dill seeds
2 garlic cloves, slivered
dill flower-heads, to garnish (optional)

MAKES ABOUT 2½ QUARTS

1 Cut the cucumbers diagonally into medium-thick slices, and set aside. Put the water, vinegar and salt in a saucepan. Bring to a boil, then remove immediately from the heat.

2 Fill sterilized preserving jars with the cucumber slices, tucking the bay leaves, dill seeds and garlic slivers between the layers. Cover with the warm vinegar mixture, filling the jars to the top.

3 Close the jars tightly, and leave on a sunny window sill for at least a week before using. Dill flower-heads can be used to garnish the pickle, if liked.

47

Rosemary Vinegar

INGREDIENTS

*sufficient rosemary sprigs to fill a 2½ cup
measure, plus extra to decorate
2½ cups distilled white vinegar*

MAKES ABOUT 2½ CUPS

48

I Initially, sterilize a wide-necked bottle or pickling jar. Place the rosemary sprigs in the sterilized bottle or jar. Fill to the top with the vinegar. Cover tightly with a suitable lid, and place in a sunny spot, such as a window sill, for about 4–6 weeks.

2 Using a coffee filter paper supported in a strainer, filter the vinegar mixture into a saucepan. Discard the rosemary. Heat the vinegar to simmering point but take care not to allow it to boil.

3 If you intend to store the rosemary vinegar in the bottle or jar in which it was made, wash the bottle or jar and its lid well in hot, soapy water. Rinse thoroughly, and dry in a warm oven. Alternatively, use sterilized decorative bottles. Place a fresh sprig or two of rosemary in the chosen container(s) for decorative purposes, pour in the vinegar, then seal tightly. Store in a dark place, and use within 1 year.

Herb Garden Dressing Mix

INGREDIENTS

1 cup dried oregano
1 cup dried basil
½ cup dried marjoram
½ cup dried dill weed
½ cup dried mint
4 tablespoons onion powder
2 tablespoons mustard powder
2 teaspoons salt
1 tablespoon freshly ground black pepper

MAKES ABOUT 5OZ

1 Mix the ingredients together in a bowl. Transfer the mixture to a clean jar, and seal tightly. Store in a dry place, out of direct sunlight, until you need it.

2 To make a batch of salad dressing, mix 2 tablespoons of the herb mixture with 1½ cups of extra virgin olive oil or sunflower oil and about ½ cup of cider vinegar. Whisk thoroughly. Let stand for 1 hour. Whisk again before using.

COOK'S TIP

When fresh herbs are not available, this dried herb mixture makes a delicious addition to soups and stews. Try sprinkling it over cooked vegetables, too, for a summery taste.

Rose Petal Jelly

INGREDIENTS

*red or pink roses with sufficient petals
to fill a 2½-cup measure loosely
2 cups water
generous 3 cups superfine or vanilla sugar
4 tablespoons white grape juice
4 tablespoons red grape juice
2 ounces powdered fruit pectin
2 tablespoons rose water*

MAKES ABOUT 2LB

1 Remove all the petals from the roses. Trim each petal at its base to remove the white tip. Place the rose petals, water and about ⅓ cup of the sugar in a saucepan, and bring to a boil. Reduce the heat, and simmer for 5 minutes.

2 Remove the pan from the heat, allow to cool, and cover. Let it stand overnight for the rose fragrance to infuse.

3 Strain the syrup into a large saucepan or preserving pan, and discard the petals. Add the grape juices and pectin. Boil hard for I minute, then stir in the rest of the sugar until dissolved. Boil the mixture hard for I minute more, then remove it from the heat.

4 Test for setting by placing a small spoonful of the hot mixture on a saucer. Let cool: the surface should wrinkle when pushed with a finger. If it is still too runny, return to the heat, and continue boiling and testing until ready. The consistency should be that of a soft jelly. Alternatively, you can test for setting-point using a cooking thermometer – jellies reach setting-point at 225°F.

5 Add the rose water. Ladle the hot jelly into sterilized glass jars, and seal at once with waxed paper circles and cellophane lids secured with elastic bands. Decorate the tops of the jars with circles of fabric held in place with lengths of ribbon.

Rhubarb & Ginger Mint Preserve

INGREDIENTS

4½ pounds rhubarb
1 cup water
juice of 1 lemon
2-inch piece of fresh ginger
6 cups sugar
⅔ cup preserved ginger, chopped
2-3 tablespoons finely chopped mint (preferably
ginger mint) leaves

MAKES ABOUT 6LB

1 Trim the rhubarb, cutting it into small pieces of about 1 inch in length. Place the rhubarb, water and lemon juice in a preserving pan. Peel and bruise the piece of fresh ginger. Bring the rhubarb and water to a boil, then add the ginger. Lower the heat, and simmer, stirring frequently, until the rhubarb is soft. Remove, and discard the ginger.

2 Stir in the sugar until dissolved. Bring to a boil, and boil rapidly for 10–15 minutes to reach setting-point (see page 50). With a metal slotted spoon, remove any scum from the surface.

3 Stir the preserved ginger and mint leaves into the cooked preserve, then immediately ladle it into sterilized glass jars. Seal at once with waxed paper circles and cellophane lids secured with elastic bands. Decorate the tops of the jars with circles of brown paper held in place with lengths of raffia.

Lemon & Mint Curd

INGREDIENTS

6 mint leaves
4 cups superfine sugar
6 lemons
1 ½ cups butter, cut into chunks
8 eggs, beaten

MAKES ABOUT 3LB

1 Place the mint leaves and sugar in a food processor or blender, and process by pulsing the machine until the mint is finely chopped. Scrape the mixture into a large, heatproof bowl, and set aside.

2 Pare the lemons thinly, taking care to remove none of the white pith. Cut the pared rind into large pieces, and add to the bowl. Squeeze the juice from the lemons, and add to the bowl. Add the chunks of butter. Finally add the beaten eggs, and mix together lightly. Bring a saucepan of water to a boil, remove it from the heat, and set the bowl over it. Whisk the lemon mixture gently, until all the butter has melted and the sugar has dissolved. Remove the lemon rind.

3 Continue to cook the mixture over simmering water, stirring frequently, for 35–40 minutes or until the mixture thickens. Pour into sterilized glass jars, filling them to the top. Seal at once with waxed paper circles and cellophane lids secured with elastic bands. Add a label, and tie short lengths of string around the top of the jars to decorate. When cool, the lemon curd should be stored in the fridge and used within 2–3 weeks.

Cakes & Bakes

Dill & Potato Cakes

INGREDIENTS

2 cups self-rising flour
3 tablespoons softened butter
pinch of salt
1 tablespoon finely chopped fresh dill
1 cup freshly made mashed potato
2-3 tablespoons milk
dill sprigs, to garnish
butter, to serve

MAKES ABOUT 10

1 Preheat the oven to 450°F. Grease a baking sheet. Sift the flour into a bowl, and add the butter, salt and dill. Now working quickly, add the mashed potato, and mix it in with enough of the milk to make a soft, pliable dough.

2 Roll out the dough on a lightly floured surface until it is fairly thin. Cut into neat rounds with a 3-inch fluted cutter. Arrange on the prepared baking sheet, and bake for 20–25 minutes until golden. Serve with butter, garnished with dill.

Cheese & Marjoram Biscuits

INGREDIENTS

1 cup whole wheat flour
1 cup self-rising flour
pinch of salt
3 tablespoons butter, cut into chunks, plus
extra for greasing
¼ teaspoon mustard powder
2 teaspoons dried marjoram
½-¾ cup finely grated Cheddar cheese
milk (see method)
½ cup chopped pecans or walnuts
butter, to serve

MAKES ABOUT 18

2 Mix the mustard powder, dried marjoram and cheese into the butter and flour mixture. Working quickly, mix in sufficient milk to make a soft, not sticky, dough. Knead the dough lightly for a few minutes until it is smooth and pliable.

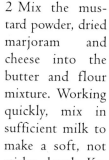

3 Roll out the dough on a floured surface to a thickness of about ¾ inch. Using a 2-inch square or round cutter, cut out about 18 biscuits.

4 Brush the biscuits with a little milk, and sprinkle with the chopped nuts. Bake for 12 minutes or until well risen and golden. Serve warm, with butter.

I Preheat the oven to 425°F. Grease two large or three or four small baking sheets with butter. Sift the whole wheat and self-rising flours into a bowl, and add the salt. Rub the butter into the dry ingredients until the mixture resembles fine bread crumbs.

COOK'S TIP

Biscuits taste better if they are made with slightly stale or hard cheese. Cheddar's creamy texture is ideal for these biscuits, but several other types of cheese are suitable, such as Double Gloucester or sharp cheddar which have equally strong flavors.

56

Rosemary Bread

INGREDIENTS

¼-ounce envelope fast-rising dried yeast
1½ cups whole wheat flour
1½ cups self-rising flour
2 tablespoons butter, plus extra for greasing
4 tablespoons warm water (110°F)
1 cup milk, at room temperature
1 tablespoon sugar
1 teaspoon salt
1 tablespoon sesame seeds
1 tablespoon dried chopped onion
1 tablespoon rosemary leaves, plus extra
to decorate
1 cup cubed Cheddar cheese
coarse salt, to decorate

MAKES 1 LOAF

1 Mix the fast-rising yeast with the flours in a large mixing bowl. Melt the butter. Stir it into the flour mixture with the warm water, milk, sugar, salt, sesame seeds, onion and rosemary. Bring together, and knead thoroughly until quite smooth.

2 Flatten out the dough with your knuckles, then add the cubed cheese. Quickly knead in the cubes until they have been well combined into the dough.

3 Grease a large, clean bowl with a little butter. Place the dough in the bowl, turning the dough so that it becomes greased on all sides. Cover the bowl with a clean, dry cloth and put in a warm place for about 1½ hours, or until the dough has risen and doubled in bulk.

4 Preheat the oven to 375°F. Grease a 9 x 5in loaf pan. Knock down the dough to remove some of the air, and shape it into a loaf. Put the loaf into the prepared pan, cover it with the clean cloth used earlier, and leave for about 1 hour or until doubled in bulk once again.

5 Bake for 30 minutes. During the last 5–10 minutes of baking, cover the loaf with foil to prevent it becoming too dark. Remove the rosemary bread from its pan, and let cool on a wire rack for at least 1 hour. Decorate it with rosemary leaves and coarse salt sprinkled on top. Eat while very fresh, preferably within a day.

Chocolate & Mint Fudge Cake

INGREDIENTS

6-10 mint leaves
¾ cup sugar
½ cup butter, plus extra for greasing
½ cup freshly made mashed potato
2 ounces semisweet chocolate, melted
1½ cups self-rising flour
pinch of salt
2 eggs, beaten
FILLING
4 mint leaves
½ cup butter
¾ cup confectioner's sugar
2 tablespoons chocolate mint liqueur
FUDGE TOPPING
1 cup butter
¼ cup sugar
2 tablespoons chocolate mint liqueur
2 tablespoons water
1¼ cups confectioner's sugar
¼ cup cocoa powder
pecan halves, to decorate

SERVES 8–10

1 Tear the mint leaves into pieces, and mix in a bowl with the sugar. Leave overnight.

2 Preheat the oven to 400°F. Grease and line an 8-inch cake pan. Sift the mint-flavored sugar and discard the mint leaves. Cream the butter and mint-flavored sugar with the mashed potato, then add the melted chocolate. Sift in half the flour with the salt, and add half the beaten eggs. Mix well. Add the remaining flour and eggs to the mixture.

3 Spoon the mixture into the prepared cake pan. Bake for 25–30 minutes, or until a cake tester inserted in the cake comes out clean. Turn the cake out on a wire rack. When cool, split into two layers.

4 Make the filling. Chop the mint leaves finely. Cream the butter, then mix in the confectioner's sugar and mint leaves to give a smooth buttercream. Sprinkle the liqueur over both layers of the cake, then sandwich them together with the filling.

5 Make the topping. Mix the butter, sugar, liqueur and water in a small saucepan. Heat until the butter and sugar have melted, then boil the mixture for 5 minutes. Sift the confectioner's sugar and cocoa into a large mixing bowl, and add the hot butter and liqueur mixture. Beat with a large spoon until cool and thick. Cover the cake with the fudge topping, and decorate with the pecan halves.

Strawberry & Mint Ice Cream Cake

INGREDIENTS

6-10 mint leaves, plus extra to decorate
¾ cup sugar
¾ cup butter, plus extra for greasing
3 eggs, beaten
1½ cups self-rising flour
5 cups strawberry ice cream, slightly softened
2½ cups heavy cream
2 tablespoons mint liqueur
4 cups fresh strawberries

SERVES 8–10

I Tear the mint leaves roughly into pieces, and mix in a bowl with the sugar, then leave overnight. This allows the mint flavor to infuse into the sugar.

2 Preheat the oven to 375°F. Grease and line a deep springform cake pan. Sift the mint-flavored sugar, discarding the mint leaves. Cream the butter with the mint-flavored sugar in a bowl. Add the eggs in stages, and beat well after each addition. Sift the flour, and fold it in. Spoon the mixture into the prepared pan.

3 Bake for 30–40 minutes, or until a cake tester inserted in the cake comes out clean. Turn the cake out on a wire rack to cool. When cool, carefully cut it into two layers with a sharp knife.

4 Wash and dry the cake pan, then line it with plastic wrap. Return the bottom layer of the cake to the pan. Spread the ice cream over this cake layer, and level the surface. Add the top layer of cake. Freeze for 3–4 hours until firm.

5 Whip the cream with the mint liqueur in a bowl. Remove the cake from the freezer, carefully transfer it to a plate, and quickly spread a layer of the whipped cream all over it, leaving an uneven finish. Put the cake back in the freezer. Ten minutes before serving, remove the cake from the freezer to allow it to soften slightly. Cut 3 or 4 of the strawberries into quarters and arrange on top of the cake, then decorate the rim of the plate with fresh mint leaves. Place the rest of the strawberries in a bowl and garnish with mint sprigs, if liked. Serve the strawberries with the cake.

Index

Beef with herby orange
   mustard, 21
Broccoli & cauliflower with apple
   mint sauce, 34

Cheese & marjoram biscuits, 56
Chicken: chicken with blackberries &
   lemon balm, 26
   chicken with sloe gin & juniper, 27
   warm chicken salad with cilantro
      dressing, 17
Chocolate: chocolate & mint fudge
   cake, 60
   chocolate mint truffle filo
      packages, 39
   iced lemon meringue bombe with
      mint chocolate, 42
Citrus mint sparkler, 45

Dill: dill & potato cakes, 55
   dill pickles, 47
   Normandy fish with parsley
      & dill, 19
   potted salmon with lemon
      & dill, 18
Duck with red plums & cilantro, 29

Green bean salad with savory, 37

Herb & chili gazpacho, 13
Herb garden dressing mix, 49

Lamb pie with pear, ginger & mint
   sauce, 24
Lemons: iced lemon meringue bombe
   with mint chocolate, 42
   lemon & mint curd, 53

Mint: broccoli & cauliflower with
   apple mint sauce, 34
   chocolate & mint fudge cake, 60
   chocolate mint truffle filo
      packages, 39
   citrus mint sparkler, 45
   iced lemon meringue bombe with
      mint chocolate, 42
   lamb pie with pear, ginger & mint
      sauce, 24
   lemon & mint curd, 53
   rhubarb & ginger mint preserve, 52
   smoked trout with minted
      grapefruit, 16
   strawberry & mint ice cream cake, 62

Normandy fish with parsley
   & dill, 19

Pear & watercress soup with blue
   cheese croûtons, 14

Pork, roast with sage & marjoram, 22
Potatoes: dill & potato cakes, 55
   potato salad with rosemary
      mayonnaise, 36

Rhubarb & ginger mint preserve, 52
Rose petal jelly, 50
Rosemary: potato salad with rosemary mayonnaise, 36
   rosemary bread, 58
   rosemary vinegar, 48

Salmon, potted with lemon & dill, 18
Smoked trout with minted
   grapefruit, 16
Spinach, walnut & Swiss cheese
   lasagne with basil, 32
Strawberry & mint ice cream cake, 62
Strawberry punch with herbs, 44
Summer fruit cake with
   heartsease, 40

Turkey with fig & mint sauce, 28

Vegetable & herb kebabs with green
   peppercorn sauce, 31

Watercress: pear & watercress soup
   with blue cheese croûtons, 14

Zucchini & carrot ribbons, 35

64